Ralph
VAUGHAN WILLIAMS
FIVE MYSTICAL SONGS
Edited by
Richard W. Sargeant, Jr.

Vocal Score
Klavierauszug

SERENISSIMA MUSIC, INC.

Five Mystical Songs

1. Easter

Ralph Vaughan Williams
Edited by Richard W. Sargeant, Jr.

Copyright © Serenissima Music, Inc.
All rights reserved.   Printed in USA

1. Easter

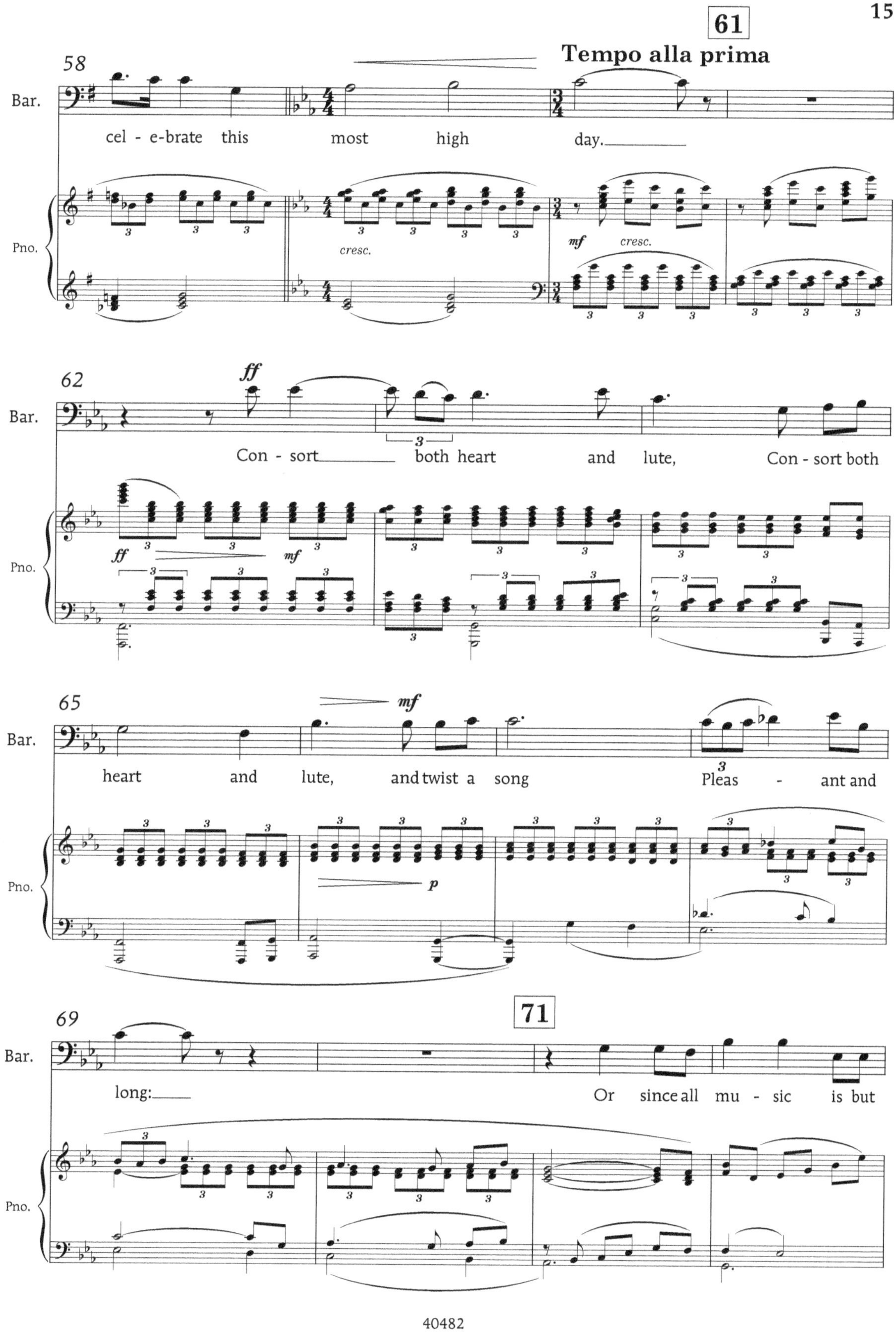
61
Tempo alla prima
58
Bar.
cel - e-brate this most high day.
Pno.
cresc.
mf
cresc.
62
ff
Con - sort both heart and lute, Con - sort both
ff
mf
65
mf
heart and lute, and twist a song Pleas - ant and
p
69
71
long: Or since all mu - sic is but

2. I Got Me Flowers

3. Love Bade Me Welcome

4. The Call

5. Antiphon

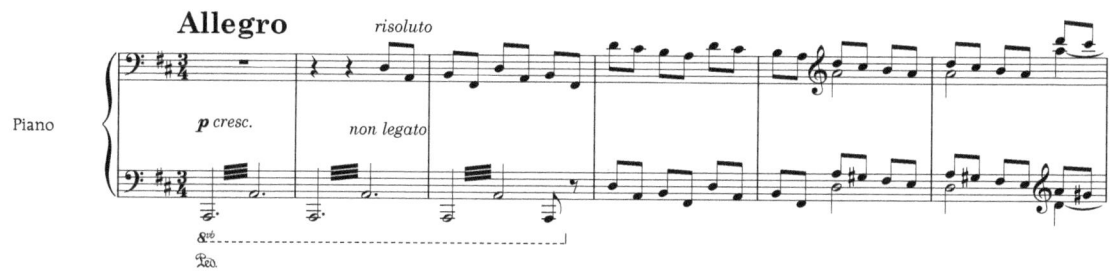

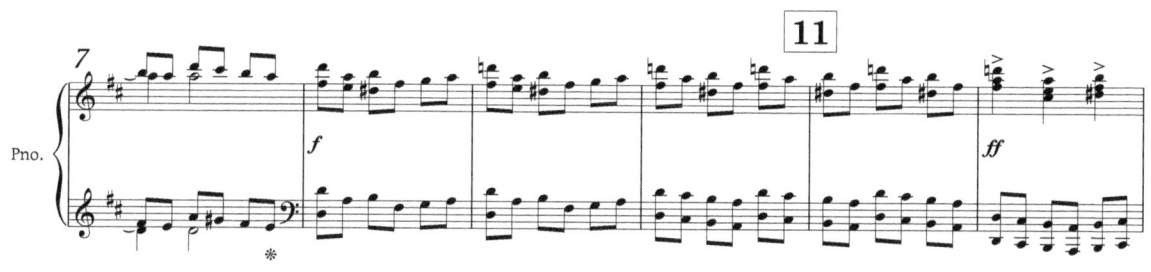

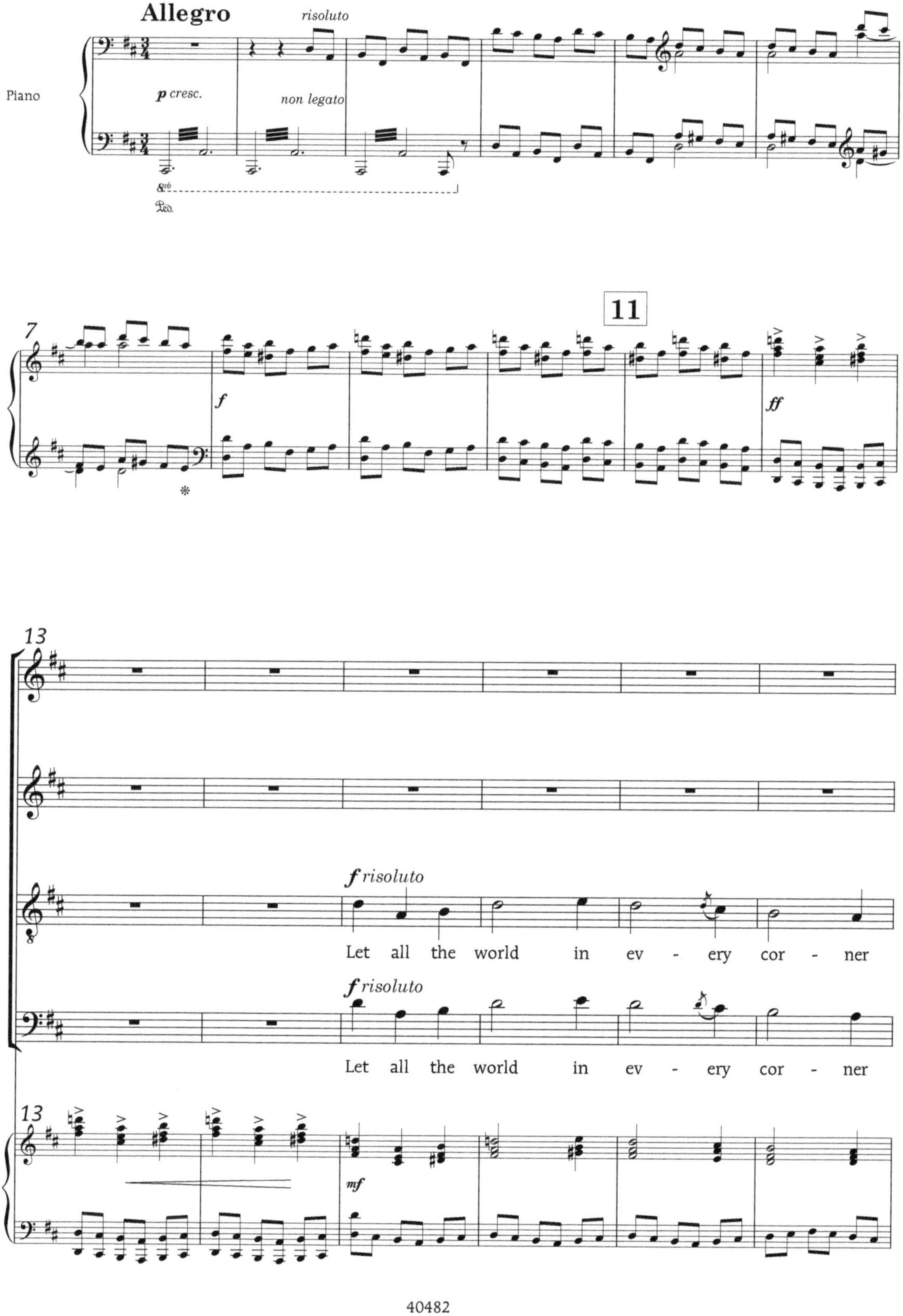
Allegro
risoluto
Piano
p cresc.
non legato
8vb
Ped.
7
11
Pno.
f
ff
13
S.
A.
T.
B.
f risoluto
Let all the world in ev - ery cor - ner
f risoluto
Let all the world in ev - ery cor - ner
13
mf

5. Antiphon

www.ingramcontent.com/pod-product-compliance
Lightning Source LLC
Chambersburg PA
CBHW081023040426
42444CB00014B/3332